OUR GREAT STATES

WHAT'S GREAT ABOUT
MINNESOTA?

✶ Nadia Higgins

LERNER PUBLICATIONS COMPANY ✶ MINNEAPOLIS

CONTENTS

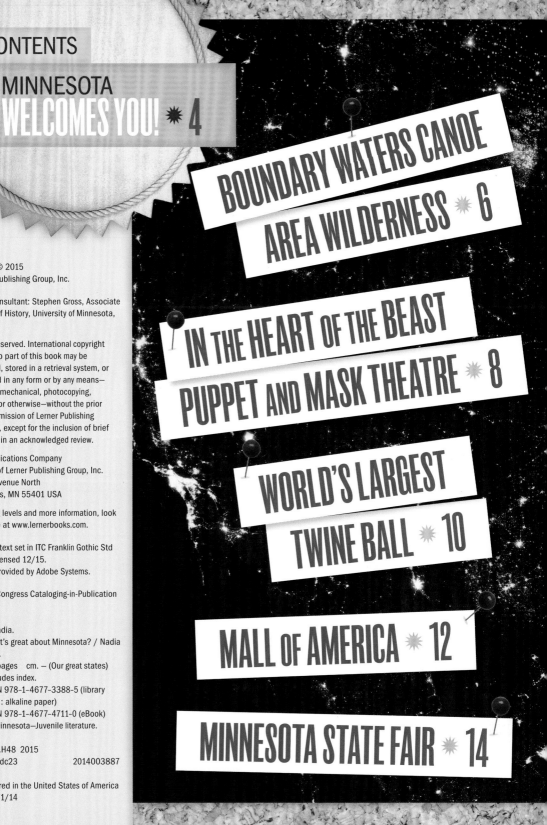
Copyright © 2015
by Lerner Publishing Group, Inc.

Content Consultant: Stephen Gross, Associate
Professor of History, University of Minnesota,
Morris

Lerner Publications Company
A division of Lerner Publishing Group, Inc.
241 First Avenue North
Minneapolis, MN 55401 USA

For reading levels and more information, look
up this title at www.lernerbooks.com.

Main body text set in ITC Franklin Gothic Std
Book Condensed 12/15.
Typeface provided by Adobe Systems.

Library of Congress Cataloging-in-Publication
Data

Higgins, Nadia.
    What's great about Minnesota? / Nadia
Higgins.
        pages   cm. — (Our great states)
    Includes index.
    ISBN 978-1-4677-3388-5 (library
binding : alkaline paper)
    ISBN 978-1-4677-4711-0 (eBook)
    1. Minnesota—Juvenile literature.
I. Title.
F606.3.H48 2015
977.6—dc23   2014003887

Manufactured in the United States of America
2 - PC - 8/1/14

Minnesota Welcomes You!

Welcome to the Land of 10,000 Lakes! In this state, lakes sparkle under open skies. Farmland stretches for miles. In dark forests, wolves howl at the moon. Minnesota is a playground for outdoor lovers. Even in the snow, you'll see people out and about. They may even wear shorts in winter! More than half of Minnesotans live in and around Minneapolis and Saint Paul. The Twin Cities are famous for their tree-filled parks. Downtown, skyscrapers tower next to old stone buildings. You'll find world-class theater in the Twin Cities. Check out a funky bookstore. Grab a cupcake from a food truck. Walk down Lake Street, and count how many languages you hear. There's so much to explore in Minnesota! Read on to discover ten things that make the state great.

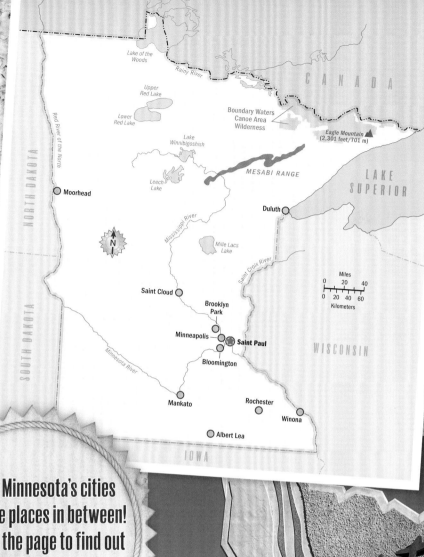

Explore Minnesota's cities and all the places in between! Just turn the page to find out all about the LAND OF 10,000 LAKES. >

Minnesota

Welcomes You

BOUNDARY WATERS
CANOE AREA WILDERNESS

> Wilderness rules in the Boundary Waters in northern Minnesota. Here, there are no roads, no buildings, no electricity, and no crowds. The only sounds you might hear are those of birds, wind, and water. More than one thousand lakes, rivers, and streams sparkle among the pines. You've never smelled air so fresh!

Fishers and canoers love this place. Boundary Waters trips are hard work, though. You must purify your own drinking water. Get ready to carry your gear on your back. There are no cars to take your tent, food, toilet paper, and garbage to and from your campsite.

But the hard work is worth the adventure. Drop a line in one of the lakes. Maybe you'll catch a walleye! Make a small raft out of sticks. Then sail it from your canoe. Are you good at finding your way in new places? You can be in charge of the compass.

At night, stars fill the sky. Stay up late, and gaze at them for hours. You will come home tired but wishing for more time in the wilderness.

Set up camp on the shore of a lake. You'll fall asleep listening to the call of the loons.

MINNESOTA BIOMES

Minnesota has four main biomes, or natural regions. Forests with leafy trees cover the southeast. Prairie grasses stretch along the western border. In the northwest lies mixed prairie and woodland. The Boundary Waters is part of Minnesota's northern evergreen forests. The trees keep their needles all through winter. Bears, moose, and wolves roam these sweet-smelling woods.

IN THE HEART OF THE BEAST PUPPET AND MASK THEATRE

> Do you like puppet shows? Visit In the Heart of the Beast Puppet and Mask Theatre in Minneapolis. You'll find all types of puppets here! Huge creatures dance across the stage. Birds fly by on sticks or strings. Handheld puppets pop out from a suitcase. Some puppets appear as shadows on a cloth.

Artists make many of the puppets at the theater. Come and join in the fun. Use water, flour, a newspaper, and paint to make your own mask or puppet. In spring, show it off at the theater's MayDay Parade. You'll see the streets come alive with puppets!

At In the Heart of the Beast Puppet and Mask Theatre, you'll see all kinds of puppets, from spooky skeletons to birds.

MINNESOTA THEATER

Minnesota is a destination for theater lovers in the Midwest. The Twin Cities have more theater seats per person than any other city outside of New York. The world-famous Guthrie Theater (*left*) is a Minneapolis landmark. Chanhassen boasts the nation's largest dinner theater. The Old Log Theater in Excelsior first opened in 1940. It is one of the oldest theaters in the nation.

WORLD'S LARGEST TWINE BALL

> Do you like weird wonders? Then the town of Darwin is a must-see stop on your Minnesota trip! In 1950, Darwin's Francis Johnson had an idea. It started with a piece of twine. He began rolling up the twine. Johnson wondered how big his twine ball could grow. For the next twenty-nine years, he rolled twine for four hours a day, every day. His creation grew to be 12 feet (3.7 meters) wide!

Today, visitors flock to the town of Darwin to stare at the World's Largest Twine Ball (rolled by one man). This amazing ball sits in a special hut. If you're lucky, a guide will let you in to touch it. Afterward, swing by the gift shop. You can buy your own mini twine ball.

Make sure to come back in August for Twine Ball Day. Celebrate the twine ball with a parade, music, and more. Bring your earplugs for the big and noisy tractor pull. See who wins the prize for the most powerful tractor.

The twine ball is kept under a roof and behind glass to protect it from wind, rain, and snow.

Francis Johnson poses with his twine ball in 1978.

MALL OF AMERICA

> Bloomington's Mall of America (MOA) is the biggest mall in the country. But just how big is it? The mall has more than 520 stores and about fifty restaurants. But that's not all! MOA is home to a fourteen-screen movie theater and an amusement park. It even has an aquarium. MOA is practically an indoor city. Seven baseball stadiums would fit inside the mall!

Are you a juggling fan? MOA has a store for that. What about fancy dog treats or funny hats? This mall has it all! Don't forget to stop by the giant robot at the Lego store. Then you can watch dolls get their hair styled at the American Girl store.

After that, scream yourself silly on the roller coasters at the Nickelodeon Universe theme park. Then mellow out with the stingrays at Sea Life Minnesota Aquarium. In the ocean tunnel, an underwater world surrounds you. Bring your sleeping bag. If you plan ahead, you can have a sleepover inside the tunnel. Drift off to sleep as sharks swim above you.

The Lego store has thousands of Lego pieces to build your own creations.

Pet the stingrays in the touch pool of Sea Life.

MINNESOTA STATE FAIR

> More than 1.5 million people flock to the Minnesota State Fair each summer. In just twelve days, guests eat 10 million chocolate chip cookies. About 20,000 gallons (76,000 liters) of milk are drunk! It's no wonder people call the fair the Great Minnesota Get-Together.

The state fair is a blast of food, rides, art, shows, and farming contests. It's your chance to eat a fried candy bar on a stick. Zip down the huge slide. Then watch someone carve a princess's head in a block of butter.

Do you like farm animals? See cattle, sheep, rabbits, and other animals. Check out the state's largest pig. Become an expert on pintos at the horse barn. Finally, head to the CHS Miracle of Birth Center. Watch newborn calves stand for the first time. See piglets snuggle up to their mother. About 170 animals begin their lives at the Minnesota State Fair each year.

MINNESOTA FARMS

Minnesota has some of the best soil in the world. Starting in the mid-1800s, settlers from the eastern states and Europe came to work the rich land. At one time, prairies and forests covered the state. Settlers cleared the land to make room for farms. Today, farms cover about half the state. Minnesota's top two crops are corn and soybeans. Hogs and cattle are the top livestock.

Enjoy fried foods, such as cheese curds, while you're walking around the fairgrounds.

BRAINERD ICE FISHING EXTRAVAGANZA

> Are you looking for a fun activity in the dead of winter? Look no further than Brainerd. Here, temperatures can fall to well below zero. Freezing winds often whip. Gull Lake may be covered by 2 feet (0.6 m) of ice. But the locals couldn't be happier. It's time for the world's largest ice-fishing contest!

Brainerd Jaycees $150,000 Ice Fishing Extravaganza attracts anglers from across the country. Ice fishing is like regular fishing. But you sit on a bucket or a chair instead of a boat. Then just drop your line through a hole in the ice. Special grips on your shoes keep you from slipping. Be sure to bundle up! You'll need two or three layers of clothing to stay toasty.

On the big day, more than twelve thousand anglers stream onto Gull Lake. At noon, their lures drop. Fishers who snag the 150 biggest fish get a prize. They might win a truck, a snowmobile, or an ATV (all-terrain vehicle). Could your family be a big winner? Good luck!

Walleye (*below*) are common in Minnesota lakes.

MINNESOTA'S LARGEST LAKE

Lake Superior borders Minnesota in the northeastern part of the state. It is the biggest freshwater lake in the world as measured by surface area. The Port of Duluth-Superior is on the west end of the lake and is the busiest port on the Great Lakes. Duluth is the fourth-largest city in Minnesota.

JEFFERS PETROGLYPHS HISTORIC SITE

> Visiting the Jeffers Petroglyphs near Comfrey is like looking back in time. Some of the rock carvings at Jeffers Petroglyphs date back five thousand years!

Long ago, American Indians recorded their life stories on huge rocks in the prairie. They carved pictures of weapons, animals, and more. You can see the carvings by hiking the site's trails.

Come when the sun is low in the sky. The carvings seem to glow. You'll see a big, shiny rock along the trail. For thousands of years, bison have used this rock to rub off their coarse winter fur.

After your hike, head to the visitor's center. Here, you'll have a chance to carve a stone arrowhead. Or make your own atlatl. Hunters used this tool to throw spears before they had the bow and arrow. Learn to throw your weapon at a bison target. Here's a hint. You'll need to hurl it overhand like a baseball. Only about fifty people hit the target each year. Will you be one of the lucky ones?

Read the signs explaining the petroglyphs.

MINNESOTA'S AMERICAN INDIAN ROOTS

The first people arrived in Minnesota about nine thousand years ago. These early people survived by hunting bison and fishing. As time went on, they learned to make pottery. They farmed corn, squash, and beans and gathered wild rice. The American Indians used Minnesota's many rivers for trade. The Dakota lived throughout much of the state, including the prairies of the southwest. In the 1700s, Ojibwa moved into the northern forests. Today, American Indians make up slightly more than 1 percent of Minnesota's population.

KARMEL SQUARE SOMALI MALL

> The Somali Mall in Minneapolis is a great place to experience an ancient culture. This mall is set up like an African market. Minnesota is home to the largest community of Somali people outside of Africa. For them, the busy mall feels like home.

One afternoon at the mall gives you a taste of Somali culture. You'll walk down halls lined with scarves. You'll squeeze past shelves of perfume. The food court features sweet tea and rice.

Few people use English at the mall. They speak their native language instead. In the coffee shop, men watch soccer on TV. Women in head scarves run many of the shops.

Soon the Muslim call to prayer comes over the loud speaker. The mall becomes quiet as Muslims perform their daily prayers. After prayer time, Karmel Square is buzzing again with life.

Hamdi Cafe ○

Girls decorate their hands with a natural dye called henna at the mall.

Choose from many colorful scarves at the different booths.

RAPTOR CENTER

> True or false? A great horned owl can hear a mouse moving under 1 foot (0.3 m) of snow. True! At the Raptor Center, you can learn more surprising facts about owls, hawks, and other birds of prey.

This center at the University of Minnesota is not a zoo. It's a hospital for feathered hunters. Each year, the center treats more than seven hundred birds. In the spring and fall, the center releases the birds. People gather to watch the release. You won't want to miss seeing the birds fly into nature.

On most weekends, you have a chance to meet the center's birds. The birds perch on their handlers' arms. Each bird has its own story. Take Annie the falcon, for example. A car hit her, and it damaged her eyesight. Annie and other raptors help teach people how to save Minnesota's most majestic birds.

Most birds are released back into the wild once they are healed.

Great horned owls are just
one kind of bird you might
see at the Raptor Center.

FORT SNELLING

Watch the white smoke billow after soldiers fire the cannon.

> Cover your ears! The cannon is about to blast. Boom! White smoke billows into the sky. Here at Fort Snelling in Saint Paul, state history comes alive. Actors show what life was like when settlers built the fort in the 1820s.

If you're not careful, you'll be put to work. Women need help with the laundry. Stir the wash with a paddle. Watch a blacksmith heat an iron rod. He'll hammer the tip into a nail. Soldiers show guests how to fire a musket. They might make you march too. Don't miss a step! At the hospital, check out the tool settlers used to pull a tooth. Ouch!

Don't leave without climbing the Round Tower. This is the state's oldest building. Take in a view of the fort through the small windows. Think about how different life was in the great state of Minnesota.

YOUR TOP TEN!

Did you have fun touring ten great places to visit in Minnesota? There's plenty more to see! Now it's time to think about what your Minnesota top ten list would include. What about Target Field, the baseball stadium for the Minnesota Twins? Or how about Lake Itasca, the source of the mighty Mississippi River? Think of ten places you want to include on your Minnesota vacation. Make your own list. You can even make it into a book with your own pictures!

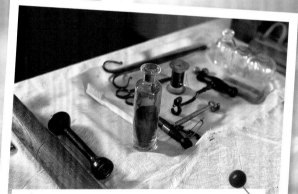

You'll see medical instruments from the 1820s when you visit Fort Snelling's hospital.

MINNESOTA BY MAP

CANADA

Lake of the Woods

Rainy River

N

Upper Red Lake

Lower Red Lake

Boundary Waters Canoe Area Wilderness

Eagle Mountain (2,301 feet/701 m)

Lake Winnibigoshish

MESABI RANGE

LAKE SUPERIOR

NORTH DAKOTA

Red River of the North

Leech Lake

Moorhead

Duluth

Brainerd Jaycees $150,000 Ice Fishing Extravaganza (Brainerd)

Mississippi River

Mille Lacs Lake

Saint Croix River

WISCONSIN

Saint Cloud

Brooklyn Park

In the Heart of the Beast Puppet and Mask Theatre

Karmel Square Somali Mall

World's Largest Twine Ball (Darwin)

Minneapolis

Bloomington

Saint Paul

SOUTH DAKOTA

Minnesota River

Mall of America

Minnesota State Fair

Fort Snelling

Raptor Center

Jeffers Petroglyphs Historic Site (Comfrey)

Mankato

Rochester

Winona

Albert Lea

Miles
0   20   40

0   20   40   60
Kilometers

IOWA

⭐ Capital city

⭕ City

⭕ Point of interest

▲ Highest elevation

—··— International border

—·— State border

MINNESOTA

Visit www.lerneresource.com to learn more about the state flag of Minnesota.

MINNESOTA FACTS

NICKNAMES: the North Star State, the Gopher State, Land of 10,000 Lakes

SONG: "Hail! Minnesota" by Truman E. Rickard and Arthur E. Upson

MOTTO: *L'Etoile du Nord*, or "Star of the North"

> **FLOWER:** showy lady's slipper

TREE: Norway pine

BIRD: common loon

ANIMAL: walleye

> **FOODS:** honeycrisp apple, milk, morel mushroom, wild rice

DATE AND RANK OF STATEHOOD: May 11, 1858; the 32nd state

> **CAPITAL:** Saint Paul

AREA: 84,389 square miles (218,566 sq. km)

AVERAGE JANUARY TEMPERATURE: 8°F (–13°C)

AVERAGE JULY TEMPERATURE: 70°F (21°C)

POPULATION AND RANK: 5,379,139, 21st (2012)

MAJOR CITIES AND POPULATIONS: Minneapolis (392,880), Saint Paul (290,770), Rochester (108,992), Duluth (86,211), Bloomington (86,033)

NUMBER OF US CONGRESS MEMBERS: 8 representatives, 2 senators

NUMBER OF ELECTORAL VOTES: 10

NATURAL RESOURCES: iron ore, lumber

> **AGRICULTURAL PRODUCTS:** cattle, corn, hogs, milk, soybeans, sugar beets

MANUFACTURED GOODS: computer and electronic products, machinery, medical equipment, processed foods

STATE HOLIDAYS AND CELEBRATIONS: Minnesota State Fair

GLOSSARY

angler: a person who fishes

atlatl: a sticklike tool ancient hunters used to throw a spear

ATV: a vehicle that looks like a motorcycle with four large wheels

biome: a distinct natural region

bison: a large, shaggy animal, also known as a buffalo, with a huge head and short horns

blacksmith: a person who crafts horseshoes and other iron objects using fire and hand tools

cattle: cows, bulls, and steer raised on farms for milk and meat

compass: a tool people use to find their way

evergreen: a tree with leaves that stay green and don't fall off in winter

musket: a gun with a long barrel, often used by soldiers in the 1700s and the 1800s

petroglyph: a picture carved in rock, often by ancient people

pinto: a type of horse that has patches or spots of two or more colors

prairie: a large, flat area with tall grasses and few trees

purify: to make something clean

raptor: a bird that hunts, such as an owl, a falcon, a hawk, or an eagle

twine: strong string made of one or more strands of string twisted together

FURTHER INFORMATION

Brill, Marlene Targ. *Minnesota*. New York: Marshall Cavendish Benchmark, 2011. Use this fun, fact-packed book for reports or for planning a trip. Learn about Minnesota geography, history, culture, and more.

BWCA.net: Your Boundary Waters Guide
http://www.bwca.net/webcams/bwca-ely-webcams
Visit this website to see what's happening at the Boundary Waters. Ten live video streams offer up-to-the-second views of the Boundary Waters, as well as the nearby International Wolf Center.

Heos, Bridget. *Ice Fishing*. New York: Rosen, 2012. Read this book to learn the basics of ice fishing, including the type of fish you can catch and safety tips.

Mingo's Guide to Minnesota
http://mn.gov/governor/dayton/mingo.jsp
Let the governor's dog teach you about Minnesota's faces and places. You'll find official Minnesota websites for students. This is a great first stop for research.

Minnesota Historical Society: Students
http://education.mnhs.org/students
This research website is designed just for kids. Click around for oral histories, timelines, and fascinating articles about Minnesota's past.

Savage, Jeff. *Adrian Peterson*. Minneapolis: Lerner Publications Company, 2011. Football is one of Minnesota's most popular sports. Check out this book to learn about one of the Minnesota Vikings' most famous football players.

INDEX

PHOTO ACKNOWLEDGMENTS

The images in this book are used with the permission of: © Wildnerdpix/Shutterstock Images, pp. 1, 6–7, 7 (top); © Rudy Balasko /Shutterstock Images, p. 4; © Laura Westlund /Independent Picture Service, pp. 5 (top), 26–27; © spirit of america/Shutterstock Images, p. 5 (bottom); © Critterbiz/ Shutterstock Images, p. 7 (bottom); © Dawn Villella/AP Images, pp. 8–9; © Steve Skjold /Alamy, p. 9 (top); © Plume Photography /Shutterstock Images, p. 9 (bottom); © Matthew Sachs, pp. 10–11; © Bettmann /Corbis, p. 11; © Jeffrey J. Coleman /Shutterstock Images, pp. 12, 12–13; © Eye Ubiquitous/Glow Images, p. 13; © Karen Gentry/Shutterstock Images, p. 14; © miker /Shutterstock Images, pp. 14–15; © Greg Benz/Shutterstock Images, p. 15; © Bruce Bisping/MCT/Newscom, pp. 16–17; © Dcwcreations/iStockphoto, p. 17 (bottom); © Dan Iverson/The Journal of New Ulm/AP Images, p. 18; © National Geographic Image Collection/Alamy, pp. 18–19; US National Archives and Records Administration, p. 19; © Judy Griesedieck/MCT/Newscom, pp. 20–21; © spstudio.com.ua/Shutterstock Images, p. 21 (top); © Tom Wallace/Minneapolis Star Tribune /ZUMAPRESS.com/Newscom, p. 21 (bottom); © Jason Wachter/St. Cloud Times/AP Images, p. 22; © Elizabeth Flores/Minneapolis Star Tribune/ZUMAPRESS.com/Newscom, pp. 22–23; © ajtoepfer/iStockphoto, p. 23; © Karla Caspari/Shutterstock Images, p. 24; © Pete Hoffman/Shutterstock Images, pp. 24–25; © iamanewbee/Shutterstock Images, p. 25; © Atlaspix/Shutterstock Images, p. 27; © Holly Kuchera/iStockphoto, p. 29 (top); © Oliver Childs/iStockphoto, p. 29 (middle top); © Luis Rego/Shutterstock Images, p. 29 (middle bottom); © Fanch/iStockphoto, 29 (bottom).

Cover: © iStockphoto.com/wweagle, (canoes) © iStockphoto.com/LawrenceSawyer (state fair); © Ross Wilson/Getty Images, (Minneapolis); © Laura Westlund/Independent Picture Service (map); © iStockphoto.com/fpm (seal); © iStockphoto.com/vicm (pushpins); © iStockphoto.com/benz190 (corkboard).